RAIL 14 PORTFOLIOS

The 'Peaks'-
Second Series

Compiled by A. Wyn Hobson

First published 1991

ISBN 0 7110 1941 X

© Ian Allan Ltd 1991

Published by

IAN ALLAN LTD

Terminal House Shepperton TW17 8AS
Telephone: Walton-on-Thames (0932) 228950
Fax: 0932 232366   Telex: 929806 IALLAN G
Registered Office: Terminal House Shepperton TW17 8AS
Phototypeset and Printed by Ian Allan Printing at their works at
Coombelands in Runnymede, England

Front cover:
Class 45/1 No 45120 (formerly D107) heads the 12.57
Scarborough-Bangor past Sandycroft, near Chester, on
27 April 1984. *Larry Goddard*
*Mamiya 645 15mm Sekor Ektachrome 200
1/500, f6.3*

Right:
The first Class 45 to be built was No D11, which
entered traffic in October 1960. Here, renumbered as
No 45122, it passes Wigston South Junction, on the
outskirts of Leicester, with the 15.00 St Pancras-
Sheffield, on 9 April 1982. *Rodney Lissenden*
*Pentax 6×7 200mm Takumar Ektachrome 200
1/500, f6.3*

Introduction

One of the orders made for 'pilot scheme' main line diesel locomotives under British Railways' 1955 Modernisation Plan was for 10 locomotives of 1Co-Co1 wheel arrangement using the Sulzer 12LDA28-A 2,300hp engine, imported from Switzerland. At 138 tons, these were to be the heaviest of the 'pilot scheme' locomotives, and the use of eight-wheeled bogies was dictated by the BR Chief Civil Engineer's reluctance, at the time, to permit axleloads exceeding 20 tons. The locomotive design work was done at BR's Derby works, and drew upon experience with the LMS Co-Cos Nos 10000 and 10001, and the Southern Region 1Co-Co1 machines, Nos 10201-3.

The frames for the first of the 10 locomotives were laid at Derby in August 1958, and No D1 entered traffic in April 1959, Nos D2-D10 following between September 1959 and February 1960. In the meantime, an order was placed for 147 locomotives of similar design, but using the new supercharged and intercooled Sulzer 12LDA28-B 2,500hp engine, and slightly smaller traction motors designed to mixed traffic specifications, as opposed to the heavy freight and express passenger orientation of Nos D1-D10 as built. The engines were built under sub-contract by Vickers Armstrong Ltd at Barrow-in-Furness, and locomotive construction was to be shared between BR's Derby and Crewe works.

It soon became clear that an order for such a large number of traction motors and control gear was beyond the capacity of Crompton Parkinson Ltd, the chosen manufacturers. It was therefore decided to cut short this locomotive series at No D137, and order 76 sets of Brush traction gear, to be applied to a separate series numbered D138-D199 and D1500-D1513. Following a further review of orders in 1962, it was decided to end the new series at No D193, and use the remaining traction motor sets in the first 20 locomotives of what eventually became Class 47. At the time of construction, all these classes were known simply by their 'Type 4' power classification; in due course, however, Nos D1-D10 were designated Class 44, Nos D11-D137 Class 45, and Nos D138-D193 Class 46.

All the Class 46s were built at Derby. By the time construction began, the works was also building Class 25s and testing Clayton Class 17s prior to their entry into service, so the construction of the last 18 of Derby's Class 45 order (Nos D58-D67, and then Nos D50-D57) was transferred to Crewe, which had already undertaken construction of Nos D68-D137.

During construction, Nos D1-D10 were named after mountains in England and Wales, and accordingly became known as the 'Peak' class. Because the external design of Classes 44/45/46 was broadly the same, Classes 45 and 46 also became popularly known as 'Peaks' — even though subsequent namings, with one exception (Class 45 No D60, later 45022, *Lytham St Annes*), were after army regiments. Twenty-six Class 45s were named at public ceremonies between September 1961 and January 1967, the names being applied to whichever locomotive had most recently emerged from a works overhaul. Some names were taken over from 'Royal Scot' or 'Patriot' 4-6-0s, and in a few early cases the corresponding steam locomotive names were simultaneously removed.

The remaining history of the 'Peaks' is sketched out in the captions accompanying the pictures that make up the rest of this volume. Information has been drawn from a number of published sources on the 'Peaks', together with additional material and comment supplied by Fred Kerr, Colin Marsden, Michael Oakley, George Toms, and the many photographers who contributed material for the book. To all, my thanks.

WYN HOBSON
Bethesda
November 1989

After initial tests in the Derby area and on the Midland main line, No D1 *Scafell Pike* worked express services on the West Coast route between August 1959 and March 1962. Here it heads the diverted 2.40pm Euston-Manchester Piccadilly express west of Berkswell, near Coventry, on Sunday 18 June 1961.

The locomotive is in the original 'Peak' livery of BR Brunswick green, with a grey horizontal stripe near the base of the bodyside and similar grey applied to the main ventilation louvres. The nose-ends of locomotives D1-D10 were fitted with headcode indicator discs, and with gangway connecting doors for use by crews in the event of double-heading.

Michael Mensing
Retina IIa 50mm Xenon
Agfacolor CT18 1/500, f3.5

In 1962, the now non-standard Nos D1-D10 were concentrated at Toton depot, near Nottingham, and performed freight work around the East Midlands area until their withdrawal.

Nos D9 *Snowdon* and D10 *Tryfan* were fitted with non-standard ventilation louvres made of vertically-mounted thick mesh; here No D10 (later 44010) is seen passing Harringworth, on the Glendon Junction-Melton Mowbray route via Corby, with a Down train of coal empties on 27 March 1965. The locomotive is propelling a diesel brake tender, a device used in the 1960s to provide extra braking-power in heavy trains of non-brake fitted or partially fitted wagons.
Michael Mensing
Nikkorex F 50mm Nikkor Anscochrome 100
1/500, f3.2

Class 45 locomotives entering service between October 1960 and June 1961 were built with box-type roller blind indicators on either side of each nose-end, to display train headcodes. The first five locomotives of the Derby build, Nos D11–D15, were also fitted with gangway connecting doors similar to those fitted to Nos D1–D10; but these were rarely if ever used, and were in due course removed.

Here No D14 (later 45015), with its connecting doors still in place, approaches Helm Tunnel, on the climb to Ais Gill on the Settle & Carlisle route, with the Glasgow-St Pancras 'Thames-Clyde Express' on 5 June 1965.
Robert Leslie
Voigtlander Vito C
Ektachrome-X 1/500, f5.6

5

Far left:
Colour photographs of 'Peaks' in service prior to the application of small nose-end yellow warning panels, in late 1962, are rare. No D100 (later 45060) *Sherwood Forester,* the first Class 45 to be named, speeds past Coaley, between Bristol and Gloucester, with the 10.18am Newton Abbot-Bradford on 7 July 1962.
Michael Mensing
Hasselblad 1000F 80mm Tessar
High Speed Ektachrome
1/1000, f3.5

Left:
The next variant in front-end design to be applied to the 'Peaks' was a two-piece four-character headcode display placed in the centre of the nose. Class 45 Nos D32-D67 and D108-D137, and Class 46 Nos D138-D166, were built with this feature. Here No D108 (later 45012) approaches Sharnbrook summit, between Bedford and Wellingborough, with the 4.25pm St Pancras-Manchester Central express on 18 September 1961.
Michael Mensing
Retina IIa 50mm Xenon
Agfacolor CT18 1/500, f2.8

Class 45 No D24 (later 45027) heads empty coaching stock for the 12.43pm Newcastle Central-Bristol through Manors station, Newcastle, on 28 May 1962. Clearly visible behind the leading cab of the locomotive is one of the roof-mounted filler points for the train heating boiler; all the 'Peaks' were built with a pair of these at No 2 end, together with three access steps inset into the body-sides for use by crews when replenishing the tanks from platform water-cranes. The alloy covers for the filler points rarely stayed in place for long, having a tendency to be blown off at high speed.
Michael Mensing
Retina IIa 50mm Xenon
Agfacolor CT18 1/500, f3.2

Left:
In the late 1950s, the St Pancras-Manchester Central service had been augmented in order to relieve pressure on the Euston-Manchester London Road (later Piccadilly) service while West Coast route electrification progressed. It became one of Class 45's first regular main-line duties; here No D89 (later 45006) *Honourable Artillery Company* draws away from Cheadle Heath station, near Stockport, with an express on 18 September 1965.
Gavin Morrison
Pentax SP1000 Agfa CT18

Left:
Class 45s were also appearing regularly on the Northeast-Southwest route by the end of 1961. Here No D25 (later 45021) brings the 13.40 Bristol-York off the spur from the Worcester avoiding line on to the WR's Paddington-Worcester main line at Norton Junction, just outside Worcester, on 15 May 1965.
Michael Mensing
Nikkorex F 50mm Nikkor
Agfacolor CT18 1/500, f3.5

The Class 45s proved to be good hill-climbers, and this was one reason for their allocation to the steeply graded ex-Midland Railway main lines in large numbers. Here No D115 passes Ais Gill summit with the up 'Thames-Clyde Express' on 4 April 1965. As No 45067, this locomotive was the first Class 45 to be withdrawn, in July 1977, after collision damage sustained near Ilkeston while hauling a Nottingham-Glasgow train, the successor working to the 'Thames-Clyde Express'.
Gavin Morrison
Pentax SP1000   Agfa CT18

Left:
No D55 (later 45144) *Royal Signals* enters Matlock with the 14.00 Manchester Central-St Pancras express on Sunday 8 August 1965. In 1966, on completion of the West Coast route electrification, the St Pancras-Manchester Central service was curtailed; the Peak Forest-Matlock section was closed completely in July 1968, and Manchester Central station was closed in May 1969.
Michael Mensing
Nikkorex F 50mm Nikkor
Agfacolor CT18 1/500, f2.8

Left:
Class 45 No D27 (later 45028) leaves Lancaster (Green Ayre) station with the 7.17pm Morecambe-Leeds on 26 June 1963. Visible is the overhead line equipment of the Lancaster (Castle)-Morecambe/Heysham electric service, introduced in 1908 and refurbished at 6.6kV ac in 1953. All services through Green Ayre station were withdrawn in January 1966, and the Morecambe-Leeds trains were diverted via Carnforth.
Noel Machell
Zeiss Werra 50mm Tessar
Agfacolor CT18 1/250, f4

Right:
The Class 46s began entering service in October 1961, and the first 28 were initially allocated to Derby depot, for Midland main line and Northeast-Southwest route duties. Here No D148 (later 46011) waits to leave Birmingham New Street with the 12.52pm York-Bristol on 16 June 1962, shortly before the station's complete rebuilding in connection with the West Coast route electrification.
Michael Mensing
Hasselblad 1000F 80mm Tessar
High Speed Ektachrome 1/250, f5

Far right:
No D193 (later 46056), the last Class 46 to be built and the last 'Peak' to be built at Derby, arrives at Kirkconnell, Dumfriesshire, with the Up 'Thames-Clyde Express' on 3 May 1968. It carries the single-unit headcode-panel fitted to the last 27 Class 46s as built. The final few locomotives in the series also entered service with small yellow warning-panels already in place.
The late Derek Cross
Rolleiflex SL66
80mm Zeiss Planar Agfa CT18
1/250

Left:
Class 45 No D48 (later 45038) approaches Cowburn
Tunnel, on the Hope Valley line, with the 7.05pm
Chinley-Sheffield stopping train on Whit Sunday,
17 May 1964. The coaching stock is entirely LNER
in origin: a rake of Gresley teak-bodied vehicles
with metal-bodied Thompson brake vehicles at
either end. *Michael Mensing*
Nikkorex F 50mm Nikkor Agfacolor CT18
1/500, f2

Left:
Until 1982, classified overhauls of all 'Peaks' were
carried out at Derby works. For a short period in
the mid-1960s, locomotives undergoing major
overhaul were outshopped in an economy repaint of
plain Brunswick green without the original grey
stripe and grille-linings. An unidentified Class 45 in
this livery is seen here near Clay Cross Junction
with the Up 'Thames-Clyde Express' on 9 June
1968. *Terry Flinders*
Zeiss Werra I 50mm Tessar
High Speed Ektachrome 1/500, f5.6

Right:
From 1967, BR main line locomotives were repainted in plain blue livery, with locomotive numbers moved to positions behind the cab doors. Very few 'Peaks' had the small yellow warning panel applied over this livery before the decision was taken that locomotive noses should be all-yellow; here Class 45 No D22 (later 45132), with all-yellow nose, is seen north of Settle Junction with the 10.25 Leeds-Glasgow Central on 29 June 1968.
Michael Mensing
Nikkorex F 50mm Nikkor Agfacolor CT18
1/500, f3.2

Right:
By 1964, over 200 modifications were needed to Classes 45 and 46, and locomotive availability had fallen to a low level. As part of a five-year refurbishment contract signed that year with Brush Traction Ltd, the first 29 Class 46s, and some Class 45s, had their original two-piece headcode panels replaced by single units at the company's Loughborough works. Here Class 45 No D116 (later 45103) passes the closed Blackwell station, at the summit of the Lickey incline, with the 12.15 Newcastle-Bristol on 10 August 1968.
Michael Mensing
Nikkorex F 50mm Nikkor Agfacolor CT18
1/500, f3.2

Class 46 Nos D166-D193 were allocated new to Gateshead depot to work services between Newcastle and Liverpool over the Standedge route, and on the East Coast main line. Here No D173 (later 46036) leaves Doncaster with a morning Leeds-King's Cross express on 22 July 1967. Regular use of Class 46s on East Coast main line services was never widespread, and their appearances south of York were usually on relief or sleeper trains, or as substitutes for Class 55 locomotives. *Terry Flinders Zeiss Werra I 50mm Tessar Kodachrome-X 1/250, f5.6*

With the end of steam traction on BR in 1968, the need for the 'D' prefixes on diesel locomotive numbers ceased, and they were painted out. Here Class 45 No 102 (later 45140) arrives at Derby with a train from St Pancras on 29 May 1974.
Hugh Ballantyne
Leica M3   50mm Summicron   Kodachrome II
1/250, f4

Above:
Class 45 No 112 (later 45010) overtakes an unidentified Class 40, still in green livery, with the Up 'Thames-Clyde Express' at London Road Junction, Carlisle, on 17 May 1969. *Don Thomson*
Canon TL 50mm Canon Kodachrome-X 1/250, f5.6

Right:
Class 46 No 181 (later 46044) prepares to exit from the locomotive yard at King's Cross station after being refuelled in readiness for its next duty, on 15 June 1973. Locomotives of Classes 47, 31 and 55 can be glimpsed in the background. This view changed markedly in the late 1970s, with the demolition of the signalbox and the erection of overhead electrification equipment.
Norman E. Preedy
Pentax Spotmatic 55mm Takumar Agfa CT18 1/125, f8

Left:
No 175 (later 46038) stops momentarily at a signal near Chesterfield with a southbound freight on 28 June 1973. Visible at the centre of the bodyside is an additional angular ventilation-grille below the main engine-compartment grille; at one time this was thought to be a distinguishing feature of Class 46, but in fact a few of the class had been built without them, and others had theirs plated over in later years, while some Class 45s acquired them some years after construction. The presence of the small vertical louvre seen here behind the leading cab was similarly variable. *Hugh Ballantyne*
Leica M3 50mm Summicron Kodachrome II
1/125, f4

Right:
All Class 44 and Class 46 locomotives received their new Total Operations Processing System (TOPS) numbers between September 1973 and April 1974. No D2 *Helvellyn* became 44002, and is seen here leaving Toton Up yard with a southbound coal train on 2 January 1978, about 18 months after the removal of its nameplates for safe keeping.

As D2, the locomotive had been delivered with its engine experimentally uprated to 2,500hp, and its traction motors regeared to give an increased maximum speed. During tests between Euston and Liverpool, to investigate the effects on track of 100mph running, D2 achieved a speed of 105mph on seven-coach trains, and 110mph on trains of three coaches. It was finally derated to the 2,300hp of its sister locomotives in February 1963.
J. H. Cooper-Smith
Mamiya 645 110mm lens Ektachrome 64
1/250, f4

Right:
No 44003 (formerly D3) *Skiddaw* passes Trowell, near Ilkeston on the Erewash Valley line, with a southbound coal train on 17 September 1975. This locomotive was to be the first Class 44 to be withdrawn, in July 1976.
Hugh Ballantyne
Leica M3 135mm Elmarit
Kodachrome II 1/500, f2.8-3.5

Right:
No 44008 (formerly D8 *Penyghent)* heads 8E40, the 18.35 Toton-Tinsley mixed freight, past Doe Hill, near Westhouses, on 2 August 1979. The locomotive still carried headcode indicator discs, but the gangway connecting doors had by now been replaced by a sealed metal plate. 44008 was one of the last three Class 44s to be withdrawn, in November 1980, and was bought for preservation, at first on the Strathspey Railway in Scotland and later at Peakrail, Matlock. *Roger Kaye*
Pentax SP500 50mm Takumar
Kodachrome 64 1/250, f4

It was customary for most or all the Class 44s to be congregated at Toton depot at weekends, when there was little or no freight work. On Sunday 10 October 1976, however, No 44005 (formerly D5 *Cross Fell*) was on duty with an engineer's spoil train at the north end of Loughborough station, adjacent to Brush Traction's Falcon works.
Tom Heavyside
Pentax Spotmatic 55mm Takumar
Kodachrome 64 1/125, f6.3

While Classes 44 and 46 were renumbered in sequence for TOPS, the renumbering of Class 45 was a more complex process, partly tied to the creation of two sub-classes with different traffic functions. Seventy-seven locomotives were renumbered into Class 45/0, intended primarily for freight work, though some retained their boilers for a while in order to work steam heated coaching stock. At first, new numbers were applied in sequence to whatever suitable locomotives came through works for overhaul; later numbers in the series were assigned to locomotives in advance of overhaul, and applied only when it took place.

Here No 45020 (formerly D26) passes Lofthouse Colliery near Wakefield with the 17.38 Leeds-Bristol on 1 September 1975. *Gavin Morrison Pentax SP1000 Kodachrome 25*

During the 1970s, Class 45s began appearing on the Standedge route more frequently. Here No 45002 (formerly D29) climbs past Batley, near Leeds, with a Liverpool-Newcastle express on 1 August 1975.

At first, the TOPS renumbering preserved the practice of displaying the locomotive number behind each cab door, and 45002 is running in this condition. However, as can be seen in the case of 45020, opposite, the practice soon developed of displaying the number only behind the driver-side door at each end of the locomotive.

Gavin Morrison
Pentax SP1000   Kodachrome 25

Class 45 were the first main line diesel locomotives to begin receiving TOPS numbers, and 50 locomotives were converted to Class 45/1 between March 1973 and July 1975, the new numbers being applied sequentially to the selected locomotives in the order in which they came through works for overhaul. The train heating boilers were removed and replaced by Brush electric train heating equipment; and in the first instance, the Class 45/1s were used mainly to haul trains of new Mk 2 air-conditioned stock on the St Pancras-Sheffield service. Here, however, No 45143 (formerly D62) 5th Royal Inniskilling Dragoon Guards is seen leaving Wakefield with the Up 'Thames-Clyde Express', formed of Mk 1 stock, on 28 July 1975.
Gavin Morrison
Pentax SP1000 Kodachrome 25

The working of the 'Thames-Clyde Express' involved two reversals, at Nottingham and Leeds. South of Leeds the train was generally worked by a Class 45/1, but north of Leeds the motive power was generally a Class 45/0 or a Class 46. Here No 45001 (formerly D13), one of the Class 45s fitted with single-unit headcode panels during the Brush refurbishment, heads the northbound working near the site of Calverley & Rodley station on 3 November 1975. *Gavin Morrison Kodachrome 25*

Above:
From 1 January 1976, the practice of displaying train headcodes on main line locomotives was discontinued. The first of two interim measures taken pending the complete removal of headcode panels was to turn the roller blinds of most locomotives to display four zeros. Here, Class 45/0 No 45020 (formerly D26) is seen in this condition at Manchester Piccadilly on 13 April 1977, prior to departure with the 15.15 boat train for Harwich Parkeston Quay. *David A. Flitcroft*
Pentax SP1000 50mm Takumar Kodachrome 64 1/125, f6.3

Right:
The accelerated Midland main line schedules made possible from 1962 by the introduction of Class 45s remained standard for 20 years. Here No 45127 (formerly D87) passes Brent Junction, six miles out of St Pancras, with a Sheffield express on 21 May 1977. *Les Nixon*
Nikon F 85mm Nikkor Kodachrome 25 1/250, f4

After the closure of the Peak Forest-Matlock line, freights from Peak Forest to the south had to reverse at Chinley North Junction. The crew of No 45042, heading 6V23, the 18.35 Tunstead to Margam lime train, prepare to perform this manoeuvre one evening in September 1976.

Built at Crewe as No D57, this locomotive was the last 'Peak' to enter BR stock, in July 1963. Since May 1962 it had undergone tests to assess the effects of uprating the Sulzer 12LDA28-B engine to the 2,750hp of the 12LDA28-C engine then being fitted to Class 47. The uprating was eventually found not to have any significant advantages, and was abandoned in early 1964. Consideration had also been given to powering all four axles of each bogie, giving a Do-Do wheel arrangement; but as this would have raised the locomotive's weight to 160 tons, the proposal had been vetoed.
Roger Kaye
Pentax SP500 50mm Takumar Kodachrome 64 1/250, f4

A variant of the 'four zeros' headcode panel display was the fitting of a fixed blind showing four zeros of smaller size. One of the locomotives so fitted was No 45123 (formerly D52) *Lancashire Fusilier*, seen here passing Trent Junction, near Nottingham, with the 17.10 St Pancras-Sheffield express on 3 July 1977. *Chris Dyke*
Praktica L 180mm Soligor Kodachrome 64
1/500, f4

Above:
From 1980, the railway landscape south of Bedford was transformed by the electrification of the suburban service from St Pancras. Here No 45061 (formerly D101) passes Chiltern Green, north of Harpenden, with a southbound vans train on 8 April 1981. The locomotive illustrates the second of the interim measures taken prior to the removal of locomotive headcode panels: the fitting of fixed black blinds displaying a pair of large white dots illuminated from behind. *Paul Shannon*
Olympus OM1 75-150mm Zuiko at 110mm
Kodachrome 64 1/250, f5.6-8

Right:
No 45071 (formerly D125) heads the 08.28 Swansea-Manchester Piccadilly past the site of University station, then under construction in Edgbaston, Birmingham, on 21 May 1977. By this time, the roof-mounted boiler filler points and bodyside steps on all Class 45s and Class 46s had been plated over, having been replaced by waist-level filler points when platform water cranes were abandoned. *Michael Mensing*
Bronica 135mm lens Agfachrome 50S (uprated)
1/800, f5.6

Left:
The traction motors fitted to Class 46 proved t[o] have poorer acceleration and hill-climbing chara[c]teristics than those of Class 45, and this was part[ly] why the class soon ceased regular operation on th[e] Midland main line, with its steep gradients an[d] numerous speed restrictions. On the other han[d] the Brush motors had a better starting tractiv[e] effort, and this made Class 46 a popular choice f[or] heavy freight work, especially on the Wester[n] Region, to which approximately half the class we[re] transferred in the early 1970s. Here No 4602[7] (formerly D164) approaches Fairwood Junction, i[n] the Vale of the White Horse, with empty Foste[r] Yeoman stone hoppers from Westbury yard t[o] Merehead Quarry on 8 May 1979. *Tom Heavyside*
Pentax Spotmatic 55mm Takumar
Kodachrome 64 1/250, f5

Right:
Both Class 45 and Class 46 were extensively used o[n] inter-Regional services into the West Countr[y] Here No 45027 (formerly D24) heads the 10.2[?] Leeds-Paignton away from Dawlish on 17 Ap[r] 1981. *A. O. Wynn*
Olympus OM1 85mm lens Kodachrome 64
1/500, f5.6

Above:
From 1976, 'Peak' headcode panels were gradually replaced by flush metal plates containing pairs of marker lights. Here No 45056 (formerly D91) runs an Up Speedlink freight through Totnes station on 19 April 1984. Class 45s took over many freight duties in Devon and Cornwall after the withdrawal of the WR's diesel-hydraulic classes; as with Class 46, their 138 tons weight and eight-wheeled bogies gave them adhesion characteristics that made them well suited to such work, even though they were nominally less powerful than the locomotives they replaced, and also restricted, by the bogies' length and rigidity, to lines laid for heavy freight traffics. *Tom Heavyside*
Pentax Spotmatic 55mm Takumar
Kodachrome 64 1/250, f5

Right:
St Pancras station on 6 May 1978, as No 45102 (formerly D51) departs with the 17.16 for Nottingham. An unidentified 'Peak' stands at the head of another express, and No 45115 (formerly D81) awaits its next turn of duty. *Gavin Morrison*
Kodachrome 25

Left:
A further reason why Class 46 was unpopular with
passenger drivers used to Class 45s was that whereas
the latter had self-governing load regulators,
Class 46s had only manual field notching, and were
thus more awkward to drive. However, on the
Standedge route, where Class 45 was little known,
Class 46 dominated passenger workings until the
arrival of ETH-only (electric train heating-only)
stock. Here No 46022 (formerly D159) draws the
empty stock of a train from Liverpool out of
Newcastle Central station on 6 June 1979.
Hugh Ballantyne
Leica M3 50mm Summicron Kodachrome 25
1/250, f2.8-3.5

Right:
With the spread of ETH-only stock, the work of
Class 46 became increasingly restricted to freight
traffic. Here No 46047 (formerly D184) passes
Barrow Hill, near Chesterfield, with 6E69, the
10.45 Loughborough-York ballast hoppers, on
7 July 1981. *Paul Shannon*
Olympus OM1 200mm Zuiko Kodachrome 64
1/250, f5.6-8

Above:
In their last years, some Class 45s were fitted with powerful tungsten halogen headlights in addition to the pairs of marker lights at each end. Here No 45143 (formerly D62) passes Bradley Junction, near Huddersfield, with the Heaton-Manchester Red Bank vans train on 23 March 1986. The locomotive's name, *5th Royal Inniskilling Dragoon Guards*, had been revised the previous year by the addition of *1685-1985*. *Gavin Morrison Minolta 7000 Kodachrome 64*

Right:
No 45132 (formerly D22) approaches Water Orton, near Birmingham, with a Newcastle-Poole service on 5 March 1983. *A. O. Wynn Pentax Spotmatic 100mm lens Kodachrome 64 1/500, f5.6*

Above:

Class 45s took over the working of the 'Thames-Clyde Express' and the 'Waverley' (St Pancras-Edinburgh) in 1961. The 'Waverley' was discontinued in 1969 on closure of the route from Carlisle to Edinburgh via Hawick, but the 'Thames-Clyde Express' continued until 1976, when it was replaced by a Nottingham-Glasgow service over the Settle & Carlisle route, using Class 45 or Class 46 power. In 1982 this service was diverted to run via the West Coast route, and a twice-daily Leeds-Carlisle return service was substituted. Here No 45142 (formerly D83) crosses Lunds viaduct, north of Garsdale, with the 09.07 Leeds-Carlisle on 3 March 1984.
Hugh Ballantyne
Leica M4-2 90mm Summicron Kodachrome 25 1/250, f2.8

Right:

Class 46s were regularly used on secondary services between Newcastle, Edinburgh and Aberdeen. Here No 46045 (formerly D182) crosses the Royal Border Bridge at Berwick-upon-Tweed with the 07.30 Edinburgh-Newcastle stopping train, including a Travelling Post Office vehicle, on 17 April 1981. *Tom Heavyside*
Pentax Spotmatic 55mm Takumar Kodachrome 64 1/500, f4

Above:
It is not known how No D163 *Leicestershire and Derbyshire Yeomanry* came to be the only Class 46 that was named, or why, like Class 44 but unlike the named Class 45s, it received its nameplates during construction. Here, as No 46026, it passes Grantshouse, north of Berwick, with a coal train for

Edinburgh Millerhill yard on 16 April 1981.
Tom Heavyside
Pentax Spotmatic   55mm Takumar
Kodachrome 64   1/500, f4

Right:
Class 45/0 No 45056 (formerly D91) had just failed at the head of the 11.50 Glasgow-Nottingham when this photograph was taken at Smardale the same day.   *Les Nixon*
Pentax 6×7   105mm Takumar   Ektachrome 200
1/250, f11

Left:
No 46045 (formerly D182) edges past Goose Hill Junction, Normanton, with a westbound ballast-train on 23 May 1983. One of the last batch of Class 46s to be withdrawn, in November 1984, it was then transferred to Departmental stock as No 97404 and operated for a time as a test locomotive. *Rodney Lissenden*
Pentax 6×7 200mm lens Ektachrome 200 1/250, f8

Right:
The reallocation, in 1975, of a number of Class 46s from Plymouth Laira depot to Cardiff Canton, for use on freights in and from South Wales, did not prove a success, partly because the tightly-curved valley lines were responsible for an increased incidence of cracking in the plate-framed, long wheelbase bogies. 'Peaks' had long worked into South Wales on expresses from the North via Birmingham, however, and occasionally worked at least as far west as Llanelli on main line freights. In later years, Class 46s also worked on the North & West route between Cardiff and Crewe via Shrewsbury for a period.

Here No 46017 (formerly D154) draws a train out of Cardiff's Pengam Freightliner terminal on 13 September 1979. No 46017 was one of 23 Class 46s withdrawn in November 1980, following a national decline in freight traffic due to economic recession, but was also one of a number that were reinstated about a year later after an upturn in Freightliner work. It was finally withdrawn in April 1984. *Hugh Ballantyne*
Leica M3 135mm Elmarit Kodachrome 25 1/500, f3.2

Far left:
Class 46s largely disappeared from trans-Pennine services after 1980, and were replaced in part by Class 45/1s. The period that followed saw an expansion of these services, and locomotive diagrams were intensive. Nonetheless, 80% availability was achieved by the class in the early 1980s, following a programme of major overhauls at Derby and then Crewe works, lasting until 1984.

Here No 45112 (formerly D61 *Royal Army Ordnance Corps*) leaves Liverpool Lime Street with the 14.03 for Newcastle on 14 June 1986. *Gavin Morrison Kodachrome 25*

Left:
No 45119 (formerly D34) joins the West Coast main line at Winwick Junction, north of Warrington, with the 12.55 Scarborough-Bangor on 29 May 1985.
Paul Shannon
Olympus OM1 100mm Zuiko
Kodachrome 64 1/250, f5.6-8

Left:
Class 46s displaced from Northeast-Southwest route duties by InterCity 125 trains made occasional appearances in North Wales during 1981. From 1982, however, Class 45/1s displaced from Midland main line duties by IC125s began appearing on trains between Manchester and North Wales in increasing numbers; and from mid-1983, when these services were extended to the Northeast, Class 45 became the principal motive power.

Here No 45134 (formerly D126) heads the 12.53 Scarborough-Bangor across Pen-y-Clip viaduct, Llanfairfechan, on 8 May 1987, three days before all locomotive-hauled trans-Pennine workings to North Wales were displaced by Sprinter units.
Antony R. Guppy
Canon A1   50mm Canon   Kodachrome 64
1/500, f4

Right:
'Peak'-hauled North Wales services eventually operated between Holyhead/Bangor/Llandudno and York/Scarborough/Newcastle, in various permutations. Class 45/0 locomotives occasionally appeared on them in the summer months, and there were a few instances of Class 45/1s appearing on Euston expresses between Holyhead and Crewe. Latterly, Class 45s also worked some Freightliner trains on the route.

Here No 45115 (formerly D81) leaves Colwyn Bay with the 11.00 Scarborough-Bangor on 23 April 1984. On the right are the earthworks of the A55 Colwyn Bay bypass, then under construction.
Wyn Hobson
Pentax Spotmatic II   50mm Takumar
Kodachrome 64   1/250, f5.6-8

Above:
No 45037 (formerly D46) passes Washwood Heath, Birmingham, with a post-Christmas Reading-York extra on 30 December 1982. *Les Nixon Nikon F 85mm Nikkor Kodachrome 25 1/250, f2.2*

Right:
Although all principal Midland main line services were in the hands of IC125 trains by mid-1982, a few secondary services continued to be Class 45-worked until the final withdrawal of the class. Here No 45108 (formerly D120) heads north out of Leicester with the 15.40 Derby-St Pancras, diverted via the Corby route due to engineering works, on a Sunday in January 1986. *Antony R. Guppy Canon A1 135mm lens Kodachrome 64*

Left:
The last 11 years of the Class 45s' service saw their gradual concentration at a smaller number of main depots. Leeds Holbeck's allocation (reputedly the best performers of the whole class) were transferred to York in May 1978,.and thence to Tinsley depot, Sheffield, a year later. Between January 1985 and September 1986, all the surviving Class 45s were officially allocated to Toton depot, and the remaining locomotives were then reallocated to Tinsley until the class's final withdrawal.

Here Class 45/1 No 45102 (formerly D51) climbs towards Scout tunnel, Mossley, near Stalybridge, with a Liverpool-Newcastle train on 25 January 1986. *Les Nixon*
Pentax 6×7 150mm Takumar Ektachrome 200 1/500, f5.6

Right:
Late on a February afternoon in 1978 an unidentified Class 45 passes Kilnhurst, north of Sheffield, with a St Pancras-Leeds express.
Les Nixon
Nikon F 85mm Nikkor Kodachrome 25

Left:
The Buxton area was one of the last in which Class 45/0 had regular freight work; here, in the company of three Class 37s, No 45012 (formerly D108) waits at the town's small depot for its next turn of duty banking limestone trains from Peak Forest, on 27 September 1987.

In May of that year, staff at Tinsley depot had begun to apply unofficial names to all the remaining Class 45s. No 45012 acquired the name *Wyvern II*, together with painted representations of the depot's 'white rose' crest and its former shed code plate.
Peter Gater
Bronica S2A 75mm Nikkor Fujichrome 100D
1/500, f8

Right:
During the 1986-87 timetable, the Sunday 12.15 Derby-St Pancras was rostered for double heading, and sometimes produced a pair of Class 45s. No 45101 (formerly D96) and No 45105 (formerly D86) are braking for the Wellingborough stop as they pass Finedon Road signalbox on 31 August 1986; in the foreground, No 45148 (formerly D130) moves forward with a track-lifting train. Beyond the signalbox is the site of Wellingborough locomotive depot, where a small fleet of 'Peaks' had replaced '9F' 2-10-0s over 20 years previously to work iron ore trains to Tees-side. *Antony R. Guppy*
Canon A1 50mm Canon Kodachrome 25
1/500, f2.8

Right:
Class 45/0 No 45007 (formerly D119) and Class 45/1 No 45107 (formerly D43) at Scarborough after working in with Pathfinder Tours' '45 Finale' railtour on 3 October 1987. No 45007 carries the unofficial name *Taliesin*, and No 45107 the unofficial name *Phoenix*. No 45107 also illustrates the white embellishment applied to window frames on some Class 45s in their later years. *A. O. Wynn Olympus OM40 85mm lens Fujichrome 100 1/125, f11*

Left:
In the summer of 1988 No 45106 (formerly D106) was refurbished for use on the railtours, after the withdrawal of the other remaining Class 45s. It was repainted in green (actually a lighter shade than the original Brunswick green), and is seen here at Marchwood, on the Fawley branch near Southampton, on Pathfinder Tours' 'Wessex Adventurer' railtour on 5 November 1988. No 45106 was finally withdrawn in February 1989, after a fire caused by a traction motor flashover (always a potential problem for the 'Peaks' at higher speeds) while the locomotive was working a Derby-St Pancras commuter service. *Antony R. Guppy Canon A1 50mm Canon Kodachrome 64 1/500, f4*

In July 1987, five withdrawn Class 45/0s were transferred to Departmental stock, following four Class 46s and one Class 45 similarly transferred in earlier years. Here No 97413 (formerly D114 and 45066) joins the East Coast main line at Low Fell, Gateshead, with a train of spent ballast in old mineral wagons bound for Tyne Yard, on 3 March 1988. The locomotive was finally withdrawn in August 1988.
Hugh Ballantyne
Leica M4-2 50mm Summicron
Kodachrome 25 1/125, f2

Right:
The Class 44s were scrapped at BREL's Derby works between 1976 and 1980, and most Class 46s at BREL's Swindon works between 1982 and 1986. Some Class 45s, too, were scrapped at BREL works, and a substantial number at private scrapyards. Scrapping of Class 45s was in many cases preceded by periods of open storage at BR depots. Here a group of these locomotives, with No 45070 (formerly D122) prominent, is seen in the sidings at March TMD, Cambridgeshire, on 4 June 1988. No 45070 was finally cut up by M.C. Processors, Glasgow, the following November.

Four 'Peaks' have been privately preserved: Class 44 Nos D4 *Great Gable* and D8 *Penyghent*, and Class 45 Nos D99 *3rd Carabinier* and D100 *Sherwood Forester. Ian Cowley*
Pentax K1000 50mm Pentax M
Kodachrome 64 1/250, f5.6

Back cover:
Privately preserved Class 45 No D100 *Sherwood Forester* at the Basingstoke Rail Exhibition of 26 September 1987. The locomotive had been restored in as-built livery, and was rededicated on this day by members of the regiment after which it is named. *Norman E. Preedy*
Mamiya 645 80mm Sekor
Fuji RD100 1/125, f8